EXTREME SURVIVORS

Animals That Time Forgot

KIMBERLY RIDLEY

TILBURY HOUSE
PUBLISHERS

Tilbury House Publishers
12 Starr St.
Thomaston, Maine 04861
800–582–1899 • www.tilburyhouse.com

First edition: November 2017 • 10 9 8 7 6 5 4 3 2 1

Library of Congress Control Number: 2017950556

Cover and interior designed by Frame25 Productions
Printed in Korea through Four Colour Print Group, Louisville, KY

Dedication

*In memory of my brother, Kenneth J. Ridley, 1957–2016, who got me
out into the wild world in the first place. And always, for Thomas. —K.R.*

Photo Credits

Front cover, Kelvin Aitken / VWPics / Alamy Stock Photo; title page, jarous / Adobe Stock; p.3, Science Photo
Library / Photo Researchers; p.4, Kelvin Aitken / VWPics / Alamy Stock Photo; p.5 top, Kelvin Aitken / VWPics /
Alamy Stock Photo; p.5 bottom, David Shen / SeaPics.com; p.6, estt / iStock; p.7 top, Elenarts / iStock; p.7 inset,
Dennis Jacobsen / Shutterstock; p.8 bottom, Mark Moffett / Minden Pictures; p.8 inset, oldbunyip / iStock; p.9,
Haplochromis / Wikimedia Commons; p.10, bowdenimages / iStock; p.11 top, Germán Poo-Caamaño / flickr.
com; p.11 bottom, c. 1881 by Messers. Elliot and Fry; p.12 Dirk Ercken / Dreamstime; p.13 top, Sebastian Ritter /
Wikimedia Commons; p.13 middle left, brewbooks / flickr.com; p.13 middle right, Viter8 / Dreamstime; p.14, Ivan-
mollov / Dreamstime; p.15 top, Martin Fowler / Shutterstock; p.15 middle, Bill Coster IN / Alamy Stock Photo; p.16
top, blickwinkel / Alamy Stock Photo; p.16 inset, Yen-Chyi Liu / University of Chicago; p.17 top, David Fleetham /
Alamy Stock Photo; p.17 inset, Paulo Oliveira / Alamy Stock Photo; p.18, Sean Crane / Minden Pictures; p.19 top,
USFWS Photo / Alamy Stock Photo; p.19 inset, Ruth Walker / Alamy Stock Photo; p.19 bottom, LAByrne / Think-
stock; p.20, Nature Picture Library / Alamy Stock Photo; p.21, Mint Images Limited / Alamy Stock Photo; p. 22,
Morley Read / Alamy Stock Photo; p.23 top, blickwinkel / Alamy Stock Photo; p.23 middle, Rod Clarke/ JDP/ npl /
Minden Pictures; p.23 bottom, FLPA / Alamy Stock Photo; p.24, Science Photo Library / Photo Researchers; p.25,
Science Photo Library / Alamy Stock Photo; p.26, Meckes/Ottawa / Photo Researchers; p.27, Science Photo Library
/ Photo Researchers; p.28, Christian Ziegler / Minden Pictures; p.29 top, atese / iStock; p.29 inset, simoningate /
iStock; p.30, Reinhard Dirscherl / Alamy Stock Photo; p.30 inset, pixabay.com; p.31, Reinhard Dirscherl / Alamy
Stock Photo; p.32 Velvetfish / iStock; p.33 top, ArteSub / Alamy Stock Photo; p.33 middle, Stephanie Starr / Alamy
Stock Photo; p.33 bottom, Justin Hofman / Alamy Stock Photo; p.34, Windzepher / iStock; p.35 top, WaterFrame /
Alamy Stock Photo; p.35 middle, Boris Pamikov / Shutterstock; p.35 bottom, Kris Wiktor / Alamy Stock Photo; p.36,
Dennis Sabo / Dreamstime; p.37 top, para827 / iStock; p.37 bottom, Steve Bloom Images / Alamy Stock Photo; p.38,
iStock; p.39, Jolanta Wojcicka / Shutterstock

They're prowling around the planet right now . . .

. . . prehistoric beasts whose ancestors survived the catastrophes that wiped out the dinosaurs. Don't look now, but *this* one might be lurking in your backyard . . . . Who are these bizarre creatures? What can they tell us about our distant past—and even about the future?

GOBLIN SHARK
A Creature from the Deep

A prehistoric beast prowls the Pacific Ocean off the coast of Japan, lurking in the inky gloom 800 feet (250 meters) beneath the surface. Few people have ever seen this bizarre creature alive.

Ten feet (3 meters) long with a knife-like snout. Floppy jaws bristling with razor-sharp teeth. Rubbery skin that can be as pink as bubble gum. Black, glassy eyes. No wonder the Japanese fishermen who accidentally caught one in 1898 named it *tenguzame*: "goblin shark."

Sensors on the underside of the goblin shark's snout help it detect prey in the dark ocean depths.

These spooky sharks have haunted the seas for **125 million years**. They are the last living species in an ancient group of sharks. Their relatives have all gone extinct. But goblin sharks are a young species compared with other extreme survivors, creatures that are even more ancient and strange . . . .

EXTREME SURVIVAL SECRETS

The goblin shark doesn't waste energy chasing prey in its deep-sea home, where food is scarce. Instead, it lies in wait until prey comes near, then shoots its extendable jaws like a slingshot, snapping them forward and back in an eye-blink. This creates a vacuum that sucks squid, fish, and other prey into its mouth. Needle-like teeth prevent the victim from escaping, and the shark swallows its meal whole. Gulp!

Who Are the EXTREME SURVIVORS?

Like dinosaurs, more than 99 percent of all life forms have gone extinct during the 3.8-billion-year history of life on Earth. Some were wiped out during mass extinctions caused by asteroid collisions, huge volcanic eruptions, and extreme climate changes. Many simply disappeared for no reason we've been able to discover.

The impact of a huge asteroid off the Yucatan Peninsula some 65 million years ago may have ended the age of the dinosaurs.

Archaeopteryx lived 150 million years ago, weighed about 2 pounds (1 kilogram), had feathered wings, and might have been an intermediate animal in the evolution of dinosaurs into modern birds like the red-footed falcon at right.

Other prehistoric creatures evolved into very different animals from their early ancestors. For example, some dinosaurs evolved over millions of years into modern birds.

But a few strange animals have changed little in outward appearance for more than 100 million years. These **extreme survivors**—goblin sharks, lungfish, horseshoe crabs, and a few others—look remarkably like their ancient ancestors that scuttled, slithered, and swam with the dinosaurs.

Animals and plants that resemble their prehistoric ancestors are sometimes called "living fossils," but this is a myth. All life *evolves*, changing over time in response to the surrounding environment. It's just that some of these changes aren't obvious. Think of a car like a Volkswagen Beetle. It looks almost the same on the outside as it did forty years ago, but there are new features such as airbags on the inside.

What's so special about extreme survivors besides their prehistoric good looks? They give us clues about what life was like in the distant past and how it has changed through time. What's more, studying their survival secrets can lead us to new medicines and treatments for disease.

Solving the mysteries of one extreme survivor could even help us learn how to better protect astronauts, develop hardier crops, and figure out if and how life could survive on other planets!

Meeting these bizarre creatures is like zooming backward in a time machine. Strap on your seatbelt and get ready for a strange journey.

TUATARA
A Living Dinosaur?

He slithers out of his burrow on a small island in New Zealand. Rain patters on the stony ground where he waits in the darkness, as still as a stone. He doesn't even blink. But when a big, cricket-like weta hops in front of him, he moves with lightning speed, nabbing it with his sticky tongue.

With his spiky crest and gray-green scales, he looks like an iguana, but he is not an iguana or any other kind of lizard.

Tuataras can grow more than 2 feet (0.7 meter) long. They look like iguanas, but instead they're the closest surviving relatives of dinosaurs.

He is a tuatara, the closest living cousin of the dinosaurs. His ancestors flourished **200 million years ago**. Named for the Maori word meaning "peaks on the back," tuataras are different from lizards in several ways. They have two rows of top teeth and a light-sensitive third eye on the top of the head, which disappears by age 4 to 6 months. Unlike most lizards, tuataras are nocturnal (active at night). Tuataras are the world's most "chill" reptile. Unlike many other cold-blooded critters, tuataras are active at temperatures below 50 degrees. That means they do everything slowly. A tuatara's heart beats about seven times a minute, only one-tenth as fast as a human heart.

Living slowly can mean a long life—a tuatara lives up to 150 years—but it is also risky. Invasive rats and other mammals that arrived in New Zealand with humans hundreds of years ago almost wiped out the tuataras, devouring their eggs and babies. These ancient reptiles are now endangered and live only on protected islands and in small sanctuaries and zoos. The race is on to help these ancient survivors thrive by protecting them from predators and by raising baby tuataras in "headstart" programs to release into the wild.

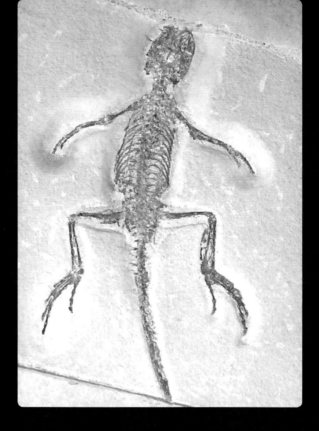

Homeosaurus is long gone, leaving only fossilized remains like this one from 240 million years ago, but its relative the tuatara lives on. Once their family, the sphenodonts, was as widespread as lizards are today.

EXTREME SURVIVAL SECRETS

Being active at night and in cool weather may help tuataras avoid predators and compete with other reptiles. Their slow metabolism provides a long life if it isn't cut short by predators, disease, starvation, or other causes of premature death.

EVOLUTION
A Long Story Short

Look around. You are related to every living thing you see. Your teacher. Your dog. That fly on the windowsill. A blade of grass. But is the human species, *Homo sapiens*, an extreme survivor? Not even close. We have only been around for 200,000 years, hardly a blink in the history of life on Earth.

Geologists think our planet formed 4.6 billion years ago. The first living things appeared as one-celled organisms less than a billion years later. We don't know yet how this happened, but we do know that all life forms *evolved* from these first microscopic organisms.

Evolution is the gradual change in organisms over many generations. It's the way new *species* develop. (A species is a group of closely related organisms that look alike and can reproduce with one another.)

English naturalist Charles Darwin developed the theory of evolution in the mid-1800s. Years of research and observations of nature led him to a great insight: Organisms that are better adapted to their environments have a better chance of surviving, producing offspring, and passing down their *traits*, or features, to the next generation.

Modern dogs are descended from wolves that were domesticated by humans about 130,000 years ago. Dogs are all one species, Canis (lupus) familiaris, *but humans have selectively bred them to create 150 breeds, including the golden retriever seen here.*

Any genetic change, or *mutation*, that better adapts an organism to its environment will tend to be preserved through later generations; any change that results in a less-well-adapted organism will tend to disappear. Darwin called this process *natural selection*, and it is the driving force in the evolution of life on Earth. All of which makes extreme survivors even more amazing. They have evolved like all living things, but they alone, of the millions of species of animals on Earth today, look much like their ancestors did hundreds of millions of years ago. Their body plans have stood the test of time.

CHARLES DARWIN WRITES THE BOOK

Other scientists—including Alfred Russel Wallace, who corresponded with Darwin—also came up with the theory of evolution by natural selection. It was Darwin, however, who compiled more than 20 years of evidence and published it in his famous 1859 book, *On the Origin of Species*. Since then, many thousands of discoveries have supported Darwin's theory of evolution through natural selection.

TADPOLE SHRIMP
Old Three-Eyes

A thunderstorm rumbling across the Utah desert leaves a pool of rainwater in the red sandstone. Two weeks later, strange creatures fill the pool. They look like miniature horseshoe crabs with forked tails. What are they, and where did they come from? There is nothing but sizzling sand for miles around.

Say hello to tadpole shrimp, the several species of freshwater crustaceans making up the genus *Triops*, which is named for the three eyes these animals all have. Their tiny eggs, called cysts—about the size of poppy seeds—can survive in dry sand and soil for many years. When downpours create pools in the desert, they hatch!

Tadpole shrimp live only 70 to 90 days and can't survive out of water. So how do they spread? Their cysts hold the secret. Some are scattered by the wind. Others "hitchhike" on the feet of animals that drink in the pools. Some cysts even travel in the bellies of ducks that eat adult tadpole shrimp carrying eggs.

Tadpole shrimp look like their fossilized ancestors from more than **250 million years ago**. Evolutionary biologists recently discovered, however, that at least one of today's species is a mere 25 million years old. (That's still ancient compared with us!) These ancient survivors are food for migratory birds, and they also help humans. How? They eat mosquito larvae!

Adult tadpole shrimp are 0.8 to 4 inches (2 to 10 cm) long.

The primitive third eye of a tadpole shrimp is nestled between its pair of more advanced (and prominent) compound eyes.

The potholes, or pools, in Utah's Canyonlands National Park are tadpole shrimp habitat.

HOW NATURE WORKS

GROW YOUR OWN TADPOLE SHRIMP

Triops kits are available at pet stores and other places. Several websites offer detailed instructions and helpful hints, including www.tadpoleshrimp.info.

EXTREME SURVIVAL SECRETS

Tadpole shrimp cysts can survive in sand and soil for 30 years, and even in the stomachs of migratory birds. This probably explains how tadpole shrimp have colonized pools in remote places such as the Galapagos Islands, more than 500 miles (800 km) off the coast of South America. Some species can produce offspring without a mate and quickly colonize new pools.

Natural Selection
IN ACTION

Like all life on Earth, tadpole shrimp and other extreme survivors have evolved through natural selection. Some changes are hard to see, because they have happened inside an organism's body or in its behavior. For example, at least one species of tadpole shrimp has evolved the ability to produce offspring without a mate, which enables it to quickly colonize new pools.

How does natural selection work? A famous example is the peppered tree moth, which lives in England. These moths rest on tree branches and trunks during the day, where they blend in with bark and lichen. In the mid-1800s, most were light gray. By 1900, however, 95 percent of the peppered moths in the city of Manchester were dark gray.

What had happened? Air pollution from factories and homes burning coal had turned urban trees black with soot and killed the lichen. Light-gray moths resting on bare, sooty branches and trunks suddenly became easy for birds to see and eat. Darker moths blended in better with the blackened bark, and more of them survived to produce dark offspring. Over time, dark-gray moths became more common in Manchester.

A light-gray peppered moth on a dark tree trunk.

Dark- and light-gray peppered moths on dark wood.

But that's not the end of the story. After new environmental laws cleaned up air pollution and soot, dark-gray moths again became easier for birds to see, and more of them were eaten. The remaining light-gray moths, which blended in with clean bark and patches of new lichen, survived more often to have offspring and again became more common than the dark ones.

If a population of light-gray moths in a clean city were separated long enough from a population of dark moths in a dirty city, the two populations might evolve into distinct species, no longer able to interbreed. Through this incremental process, over billions of years, evolution has produced the amazing variety of life on Earth today.

HOW NATURE WORKS

HOW OLD IS THAT SPECIES?

To figure out how ancient a species is, we study its fossils (remains preserved in stone), its living forms, and its DNA, which contains its unique molecular blueprint. With these and other methods, we can place a species on the Tree of Life and determine its relationships with other species—including us! We're making new discoveries about evolution all the time. In 2015, a paleontologist found a piece of feathered dinosaur tail preserved in a 99-million-year-old chunk of amber at a market in Myanmar, in Southeast Asia. His find confirmed that dinosaurs had feathers!

LUNGFISH
A Fish Out of Water

Australian lungfish.

An African lungfish walking on the bottom of an aquarium.

An eel-like fish wriggles in the yellow mud of a papyrus marsh that is drying up under the scorching African sun. Any other fish trapped there would die, but not this one.

When the watery home of the West African lungfish dries up, it tunnels under the mud. There it makes itself a mucus "cocoon" to wait out the drought until the rain returns.

Lungfish appeared on Earth more than **300 million years ago**, and they have several survival tricks. They breathe mainly through primitive lungs, rather than gills like other fish. This allows them to survive droughts that would kill other fish. Five of the six species of lungfish will drown if they can't reach the surface of the water for a gulp of air every half hour or so! Only the Australian lungfish keeps fully working gills into adulthood.

Nicknamed "salamander fish," these ancient survivors also have strange fins. The fins of most fish are thin rays of fingernail-like material covered with skin, but lungfish and their cousins the coelacanths [*SEE-luh-canths*] have real bones in their fins that are similar to those in our limbs.

The coelacanth, once thought extinct, survives in two critically endangered Indian Ocean species. Coelacanths, lungfish, and tetrapods (four-legged animals) evolved from lobed-finned fish more than 300 million years ago. Lungfish and coelacanths are more closely related to humans than to other fish.

A spotted African lungfish gets a breath of air.

In 2011, biologists observed captive African lungfish doing something amazing. They were using their skinny hind fins like legs to "walk" and "hop" along underwater structures. This discovery reveals important clues about how the first vertebrates crawled out of the water millions of years ago to live on land. Lungfish are the closest fishy relatives of *tetrapods*, or four-limbed animals—including humans. Meet your great, great, great…grandparents! Six species of lungfish live in Africa, Australia, and South America. They spend much of their time pretending to be sunken logs and sticks, waiting for unwary fish, crustaceans, and other aquatic prey to get a little too close.

EXTREME SURVIVAL SECRETS

Lungfish in Africa and South America can survive droughts for more than two years by burrowing under the mud and going into *estivation*, which is similar to hibernation. They also can survive for more than three years without eating.

HORSESHOE CRAB
A Blue Blood

A full moon rises over Delaware Bay. Hundreds of creatures emerge from the night sea and lurch onto the beach. Each has a spiky tail, claw-bearing legs, and ten eyes. Their dark, domed shells gleam in the moonlight. Are they invaders from outer space? Hardly. Monsters? Nope.

These horseshoe crabs have come ashore at sunset to spawn. A horseshoe crab uses its tail spike, or telson, to lever itself back upright if a wave turns it over.

Endangered red knots feed on horseshoe crab eggs.

Horseshoe crab eggs and a slipper shell on the sand.

These creatures are harmless. They're related to scorpions, but they don't sting. They're horseshoe crabs, and they've come to lay their eggs in the sand during the highest tides of spring. At sunrise, huge flocks of red knots arrive. These robin-sized shorebirds drill the sand for the horseshoe crabs' tiny green eggs—food they depend on to fuel their migration from Patagonia to their breeding grounds in the Arctic.

An upside-down horseshoe crab shows its claw-tipped legs, behind which are the stacked gill plates that the animal uses for swimming as well as breathing.

Many eggs remain, however, safely buried in the sand. They will soon hatch into baby horseshoe crabs—the newest generation in a line of animals that goes back some **445 million years**.

Horseshoe crabs appeared on Earth about 200 million years before the first dinosaurs. How have they survived when dinosaurs and most other ancient animals have gone extinct?

Horseshoe crab larvae develop inside their eggs, which are the size of small beads. They will hatch into miniature versions of their parents, minus the tail.

Hard exoskeletons help protect horseshoe crabs from predators, but that's just part of the story. The horseshoe crab's most amazing survival secret may be in its baby-blue blood, which contains a substance that detects bacteria. If a horseshoe crab gets a hole in its shell and bacteria enter its body, its blood immediately clots around the bacteria and seals them off, preventing infection from spreading.

The bacteria-detecting substance in horseshoe crab blood is called LAL for short, and it is used to test medical equipment and intravenous drugs for bacterial contamination. If you've ever had a shot, stitches, or surgery, you can thank horseshoe crabs for helping to keep you safe.

Male horseshoe crabs clasp the backs of females (which are larger) for spawning.

EXTREME SURVIVAL SECRETS

The horseshoe crab's blue blood clots around bacteria, stopping infection from spreading. Its tough exoskeleton protects it from predators. Horseshoe crabs eat a wide variety of invertebrates and are also scavengers, feeding on dead plant and animal tissue. They can tolerate the wide range of salinities they encounter as they move back and forth between estuaries and the open ocean.

VELVET WORM
Super Slime

A velvet worm in the Ecuadorian rainforest at night.

The spider doesn't suspect a thing. A hunter slinks toward it, gliding across the jungle floor on dozens of silent, stubby feet. She rears up and shoots streams of slime from two nozzles on her head, trapping the spider in a strong, sticky net. There's no escape.

The hunter is a velvet worm. She bites the spider and injects saliva, which turns its insides into liquid. After devouring the slime net, she sips her spider smoothie.

Velvet worms are not worms at all. They belong to a group of animals that is more than **500 million years old** called *Onychophora* [on-ee-COFF-ora], which means "claw-bearers." Their 13 to 43 pairs of feet are tipped with claws, which they can pull in, catlike, when not in use. Velvet worms today look similar to 500-million-year-old fossils of *Aysheaia* worms.

These spineless wonders are more closely related to insects than to worms, and must shed their skin to grow. And they do something extremely rare among invertebrates. Most velvet worms give birth to live young, just as mammals do, rather than laying eggs. Female velvet worms have two "litters" of up to six fully formed babies each year.

A velvet worm stalks its prey …

… fires its slime …

Physicists are trying to crack the mysteries of how the velvet worm's tiny "squirt guns" work. Their discoveries could lead to new ways to deliver medicine to disease sites in the human body.

… and moves in to consume the cockroach larva it has caught.

EXTREME SURVIVAL SECRETS

Velvet worms shoot nets of "super slime" to trap prey. They are nocturnal, which helps them avoid daytime predators.

TARDIGRADE
Zombie "Bears"

A scanning electronic micrograph (SEM) of a water bear (actual size about 0.03 inch or 0.75 mm), showing the claws with which it clings to lichens and damp moss.

They might be waddling around in your backyard right now: bizarre animals that can live for decades without food or water. Like zombies, they can even return from the "dead." Don't worry. These ancient survivors are so small you need a microscope to see them. Meet the tardigrade, also known as the water bear.

An illustration of a water bear tun, the animal's dormant form, which is not much larger than its egg.

Tardigrade means "slow stepper," named for the way this microscopic animal ambles around in damp moss like a tiny bear in a miniature forest. It looks like a chubby caterpillar with eight stubby legs tipped with claws. The largest tardigrades are just over a millimeter long, about the size of the period at the end of this sentence.

More than 1,200 species of tardigrades have been identified so far. Many live in films of water on moss, lichen, and leaf litter. Others live in ponds or in the sea. Tardigrades are found on every continent and in almost every habitat: mountains, tundra, deserts, rainforests, and backyards.

When a tardigrade's moss clump loses moisture, the animal doesn't die. It curls into a ball, dries out, and goes into a kind of suspended animation called *cryptobiosis*, which means "hidden life." Tardigrades in this state are called *tuns*. Tardigrade tuns can survive boiling, freezing, and being crushed. They blow around on the wind like microscopic tumbleweeds. When tuns land in damp moss or other moist places, they swell with water and come back to life.

Coming from a group of animals more than **530 million years old**, tardigrades are also hardy astronauts. In 2007, scientists launched tardigrade tuns into space on a satellite. They survived the vacuum of space and intense radiation that would kill any other animal.

EXTREME SURVIVAL SECRETS

Tardigrades can survive for decades as tuns, losing up to 99 percent of their water. Once rehydrated, they can repair the strands of DNA that dehydration broke.

Biologists recently discovered that tardigrades have an amazing superpower: they survive drying out by turning themselves into glass! Tardigrades have special molecules in their cells that turn fluid into glass when their bodies start losing water.

This protects tardigrade tuns until rain, dew, or other moisture brings them back to life. That's just one of the tardigrade's survival secrets. Learning more could help us better protect astronauts on space missions, develop crops that can tolerate climate change, and figure out if and how life can survive on other planets.

This tardigrade egg (shown in an SEM photo) is only 0.004 inch (0.1 mm) in diameter.

HOW NATURE WORKS

HOW TO HUNT FOR TARDIGRADES

1. Collect small clumps of moss and lichen and put them in an envelope or small paper bag labeled with the location. **2.** Soak the moss overnight (or for a few days if it is dry) in a small dish of distilled or bottled water. (Don't use tap water, which contains chlorine.) **3.** Put the dish on a piece of black paper under a dissecting microscope. Shine a flashlight sideways across the dish. Tardigrades and other microscopic animals will glow against the black background.

CHAMBERED NAUTILUS
The World's Strangest Shell

Puttering along Australia's Great Barrier Reef in its zebra-striped shell, the chambered nautilus seems mild-mannered. It's hard to believe that its ancestors were the "great white sharks" of prehistoric seas.

A sectioned shell showing the interior chambers.

More than **500 million years ago**, most creatures crawled around on the bottom of the ocean. Then ancestors of the nautilus evolved a new trick: the ability to float. This gave them an edge. They could hunt their prey from above.

Some ancient nautiluses had cone-shaped shells as long as an automobile, but the biggest ones today have coiled shells about the size of a salad plate. They live in the outermost compartment of their shells and "jet-propel" themselves along by squirting seawater through a tube called a siphon (*SY-fun*).

HOW NATURE WORKS

NAUTILUSES IN DANGER

The nautilus's beautiful shell has served it well for millions of years. Now, however, it is being overharvested for decorations and jewelry. Although it is not protected as an endangered species, harvesting is now regulated through an international agreement.

Ammonites were free-swimming cephalopods like the nautilus, and, as this fossil shows, had similar shell chambers. Yet ammonites disappeared with the dinosaurs in the extinction event of 65 million years ago, while the nautilus survived.

This chambered nautilus off the South Pacific island of Palau retreats from the photographer by squirting seawater through its siphon, which is clearly visible.

The nautilus's strange and elegant shell holds the secret to its ability to float. Inside are spiraling chambers pierced by a thin tube called a siphuncle (*SY-fun-kle*). A nautilus uses its siphuncle to change the mix of seawater and gas inside these chambers. Removing seawater allows a nautilus to float upward in the water. Adding more seawater makes it sink deeper. Like the octopus, squid, and cuttlefish, the nautilus is a cephalopod (*SEF-a-lo-pod*), which means "head-foot." Its 90 or so "feet" (tentacles) sprout from its head! Nautiluses are thought to sniff out prey with their tentacles, which have grooves and ridges to help them grasp whatever they catch. They chomp down fish, shrimp, crabs, and other prey with their strong, beak-like jaws.

Unlike squid and octopuses— its fellow cephalopods—a nautilus's tentacles have no suckers, and its eyes are more primitive, lacking lenses.

EXTREME SURVIVAL SECRETS

Ancestors of the nautilus evolved the world's first buoyant shell. These strange sea creatures are nocturnal. They hide during the day in water up to 2,000 feet (600 meters) deep and float upward into water at least 300 feet (90 meters) deep at night to feed. Nautiluses only need to eat about once a month.

COMB JELLY
Alien of the Sea

In night waters off Kona, Hawaii.

Comb jellies look like tiny glass spaceships drifting through the ocean, but that's not why they have been called "aliens of the sea." These ancient cousins of sea jellies (or jellyfish, as we call them) are so strange, they could have come from another planet.

Comb jellies range up to 5 feet (1.5 meters) long, but most are small.

A comb jelly in Antarctica.

How strange? That's a story that starts more than **550 million years ago**, when comb jellies and sea jellies were among the first animals to evolve skin, muscles, and nerves. Unlike sea jellies, comb jellies don't sting. Their "combs" are made of *cilia*: short, hairlike projections that they move like oars to swim. The waving cilia scatter light, creating rippling rainbows. Many species dangle two sticky tentacles like fishing lines beneath them to catch zooplankton and other prey. One comb jelly species, called the sea walnut, uses a set of lobes like giant lips to engulf its lunch—including other comb jellies!

But the strangest thing of all is that a comb jelly's primitive "brain"—a simple net of nerve cells, or *neurons*—is unlike that of any other animal. When the brain is removed in a laboratory, the animal grows a new one. Learning how comb jellies do this might someday lead to new treatments for brain diseases such as Alzheimer's.

And comb jellies have yet another claim to fame. They were among the earliest animals to have . . . a butt.

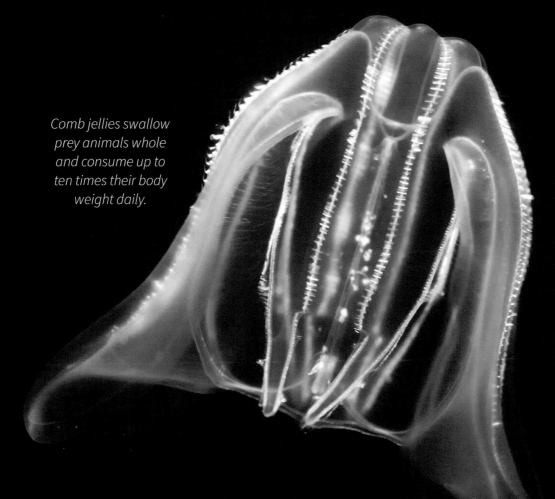

Comb jellies swallow prey animals whole and consume up to ten times their body weight daily.

Until 2015, comb jellies were thought to be like other primitive animals without an *anus*, eating and excreting waste through the same, single opening in their bodies. Then we learned that comb jellies poop through a pair of pores on their rear ends—a big surprise! Why is that a big deal? Because a separate "exit" allowed digestive tracts to develop and larger animals to evolve.

Comb jellies aren't aliens, but unraveling their secrets will help solve some of the mysteries of how life evolved right here on Earth.

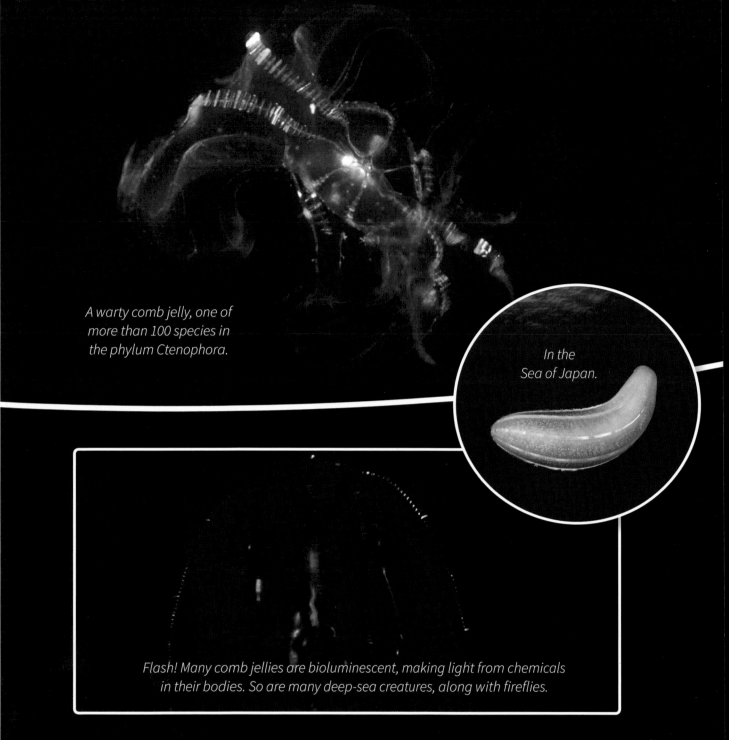

A warty comb jelly, one of more than 100 species in the phylum Ctenophora.

In the Sea of Japan.

Flash! Many comb jellies are bioluminescent, making light from chemicals in their bodies. So are many deep-sea creatures, along with fireflies.

EXTREME SURVIVAL SECRETS

Comb jellies can shrink themselves when they can't find food. They don't need mates, because they can lay and fertilize their own eggs. Some species can survive in water that is polluted or low in oxygen. They are so successful, they have become invasive species in the Black Sea.

SPONGE
Earth's Most Ancient Animal?

Sponges off the coast of Belize.

Stuck motionless on the ocean floor, sponges might seem boring. Unlike comb jellies, they have no brain at all! But these ancient survivors are the only animals that can do something remarkable: put themselves back together. If you were to grind up a piece of living sponge in a blender and pour it back into seawater, its cells would find each other, stick together, and rebuild little sponges. Yes, they're alive!

A giant barrel sponge.

Sponges are thought to be the most ancient animals on Earth. The way their cells come back together may help us understand how life evolved from microscopic, single-celled organisms about **600 million years ago**. Some cells started living together in colonies, and over eons, these colonies grew more complex, with different cells doing different tasks. Eventually these specialized cells couldn't survive by themselves, and the result was the first multicellular animal on Earth.

Sponges in the Adriatic Sea off the coast of Croatia.

EXTREME SURVIVAL SECRETS

Sponges can reassemble themselves from groups of cells. They produce more than 8,000 chemicals to protect themselves from predators and disease. Scientists recently discovered that sponges can "sneeze" in response to irritants in the water. It takes them awhile—about 30 minutes per sneeze. Ah-ah-ah, chooo....

It might have been a sponge—which could be the brainless ancestor of all animals from slugs to humans. Today, about 9,000 species of sponges thrive in oceans and fresh water from the Arctic to the tropics. They come in many shapes, colors, and sizes. Some are as tall as chimneys; others are as flat as pancakes. The smallest sponges are about the size of a quarter, while the largest anyone has seen so far is as big as a van. Found in Hawaii in 2015, it could be thousands of years old, making it the world's oldest living animal.

Tube sponges.

Sponges look like they're doing nothing, but they're constantly busy. They pump seawater through their bodies 24/7 in order to eat. Special cells that line a sponge's body cavity flick their whip-like tails in unison to create a current that sucks in water.

Other cells filter out food such as plankton and bacteria. A sponge must pump a ton of water through its body to get just an ounce of food!

As if sponges weren't busy enough, they are constantly fending off attackers. They can't bite, sting, or run away. So how do they do it? Sponges make thousands of different chemicals to protect themselves from predators, bacteria, and viruses.

Humans benefit from the unique abilities of sponges. Biomedical researchers have developed several new medicines from chemicals made by sponges, and they are studying other sponge chemicals to create better antibiotics and find new treatments for cancer.

EXTREME DISCOVERIES

It has long been thought that sponges are the world's most ancient animals, at 600 million years old. Now, however, that might be changing.

New research on DNA suggests that comb jellies may have evolved earlier than sponges, making them the most ancient animals on Earth. Scientists are still debating this, but that's not a bad thing. Every discovery about extreme survivors leads to new questions—and the chance to learn even more about the evolution of life on Earth.

All life is constantly evolving—from the planet's oldest extreme survivors to young species such as human beings. Evolution gives us Earth's amazing diversity of life—an estimated 8.7 million known species of organisms, with millions more still to be discovered.

Evolution is not just about the past or the present, it's also about the future. What scientists are learning from extreme survivors may help us treat diseases such as cancer; fight antibiotic-resistant bacteria; develop crops better adapted to a changing climate; and tackle a host of other challenges.

What else do our ancient relatives on the Tree of Life have to teach us? Scientists are hot on the trail. Maybe one day you will join them and discover more amazing secrets about Earth's extreme survivors.

A TIMELINE OF EARTH'S HISTORY

Scientists think that Earth formed 4.6 billion years ago, and the first single-celled organisms appeared about 800 million years after that. But more than 3 billion years elapsed before organisms with more than one cell appeared, some 600 million years ago. Sponges and comb jellies were among those first multi-celled organisms, and are still around today.

The top timeline on the next page covers all of Earth's history. The bottom timeline expands the Phanerozoic ("visible life") eon, which began about 541 million years ago and continues today. It includes three eras: The Paleozoic era ended with the Permian extinction, which was survived by at least seven of our extreme survivors. The Mesozoic era ended with another mass extinction—probably caused by an asteroid collision—that wiped out the non-avian dinosaurs and many other animals. All ten of our extreme survivors lived through that one! We live in the Cenozoic era.

EARTH TIMELINE

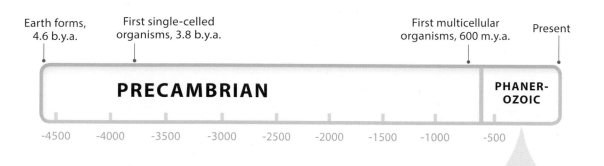

Earth forms, 4.6 b.y.a.

First single-celled organisms, 3.8 b.y.a.

First multicellular organisms, 600 m.y.a.

Present

PRECAMBRIAN

PHANER-OZOIC

-4500 -4000 -3500 -3000 -2500 -2000 -1500 -1000 -500

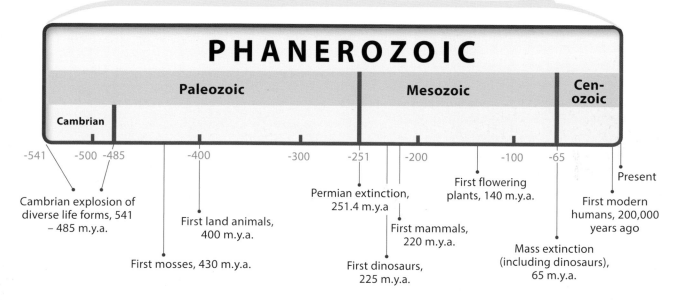

PHANEROZOIC

Paleozoic

Mesozoic

Cen-ozoic

Cambrian

-541 -500 -485 -400 -300 -251 -200 -100 -65

Cambrian explosion of diverse life forms, 541 – 485 m.y.a.

First land animals, 400 m.y.a.

First mosses, 430 m.y.a.

Permian extinction, 251.4 m.y.a

First dinosaurs, 225 m.y.a.

First mammals, 220 m.y.a.

First flowering plants, 140 m.y.a.

Mass extinction (including dinosaurs), 65 m.y.a.

Present

First modern humans, 200,000 years ago

b.y.a. = billions of years ago   **m.y.a. = millions of years ago**

SPONGE
600 m.y.a.

COMB JELLY
550+ m.y.a.

TARDIGRADE
530 m.y.a.

CHAMBERED NAUTILUS
500+ m.y.a.

VELVET WORM
500 m.y.a.

HORSESHOE CRAB
445 m.y.a.

LUNGFISH
300+ m.y.a.

TADPOLE SHRIMP
250 m.y.a.

TUATARA
200 m.y.a.

GOBLIN SHARK
125 m.y.a.

EXTREME SURVIVORS:
Up Close and Personal

Goblin Shark

Scientific name: *Mitsukurina owstoni*

Size: Adults are 10 to 18 feet (3 to 6 meters) long.

Range: Off the coast of Japan, but has been found in Australia, New Zealand, southern Africa, Spain, Florida, and Southern California.

Habitat: Rocky reefs, usually in water 200 to 920 feet (60 to 280 meters) deep.

What it eats: Squid, small fish, and crabs.

What eats it: Unknown

Appeared on Earth: 125 million years ago.

Lifespan: Unknown

Tuatara

Scientific name: *Sphenodon* ("wedge-tooth")

Size: Adults range from 12 to 30 inches (0.33 to 0.8 m) long and weigh between half a pound and 2.5 pounds (0.2 to 1.1 kg).

Range: About 35 islands off New Zealand, and in a few New Zealand sanctuaries.

Habitat: Coastal and scrub forests with loose soil for burrowing.

What it eats: Insects and other invertebrates. Occasionally young tuataras.

What eats it: Invasive rats and other mammals.

Appeared on Earth: About 200 million years ago.

Lifespan: More than 100 years.

Tadpole Shrimp

Scientific name: *Triops* ("three-eyes"); about 30 species have been identified so far.

Size: From less than 1 inch to 4 inches (20 to 100 mm) long.

Range: Various species live in North America, South America, Japan, Australia, the United Kingdom (endangered), and the Arctic.

Habitat: Seasonal pools, ponds, and other temporary wetlands.

What it eats: Decaying plant and animal matter, plankton, algae, mosquito larvae.

What eats it: Wild ducks, herons, and other migratory waterbirds; wood frogs.

Appeared on Earth: Ancestors of tadpole shrimp appeared more than 250 million years ago.

Lifespan: Up to 70 days in the wild and 90 days in captivity.

Lungfish

Scientific name: There are six species of lungfish included in a group called Dipnoi.

Size: Adults range from 2 feet to 7 feet (0.6 to 2.2 m) long, depending on the species.

Range: Sub-Saharan Africa, Australia, and South America.

Habitat: Tropical freshwater marshes, rivers, swamps, and ponds.

What it eats: Fish, crustaceans, worms, insects, mollusks, and plants.

What eats it: Mammals and larger fish eat juvenile lungfish. Adult lungfish have few predators other than humans.

Appeared on Earth: More than 300 million years ago.

Lifespan: More than 100 years in captivity.

Horseshoe Crab

Scientific name: *Limulus polyphemus*

Size: Females grow up to 19 inches (0.6 m) and males up to 15 inches (0.4 m) long.

Range: U.S. Atlantic coast from Maine to Florida, and the Gulf Coast to the Yucatan Peninsula in Mexico. Three additional species of horseshoe crab are found in Southeast Asia.

Habitat: Estuaries and bays in water less than 100 feet deep.

What it eats: Small shellfish, worms, fish, dead animal matter, and algae

What eats it: Sharks and sea turtles.

Appeared on Earth: About 445 million years ago.

Lifespan: Up to 40 years.

Velvet Worm

Scientific name: *Onychophora* ("claw-bearer").

About 200 species have been identified so far.

Size: Less than 1 inch (25 mm) up to 8 inches (200 mm) long.

Range: Australia and New Zealand, Central and South America, Africa, Southeast Asia.

Habitat: Rotting logs and leaf litter in damp tropical forests.

What it eats: Termites and other insects, spiders, small invertebrates.

What eats it: Spiders, centipedes, rodents, birds, and snakes.

Appeared on Earth: Ancestors of velvet worms appeared more than 500 million years ago.

Lifespan: Up to 6 years.

Tardigrade / Water Bear

Scientific name: *Tardigrade* ("slow walker"). About 1,150 species have been identified so far.

Size: Microscopic to 1 millimeter.

Range: Worldwide, on every continent.

Habitat: Often damp moss and lichen, but also deep in the ocean, on mountaintops and tundra, in backyards and deserts.

What it eats: Fluids of plant and animal cells, bacteria, and tiny organisms including other tardigrades.

What eats it: Amoebas, nematodes, and other tardigrades.

Appeared on Earth: Ancestors of tardigrades appeared about 530 million years ago.

Lifespan: Tardigrade tuns can survive for more than 100 years.

Chambered Nautilus

Scientific name: *Nautilus* sp. There are seven species.

Size: About 8 inches (200 mm) in diameter.

Range: Tropical Pacific Ocean from Australia to Indonesia.

Habitat: Reefs in water 300 to 2,000 feet (90 to 600 m) deep.

What it eats: Shrimp, crabs, fish, and dead animals.

What eats it: Sharks, octopuses, sea turtles, and trigger fish.

Appeared on Earth: More than 500 million years ago.

Lifespan: More than 15 years.

Comb Jelly

Scientific name: *Ctenophora* ("comb bearer"). Scientists have identified about 150 species.

Size: A few millimeters to more than 4 feet (1.2 m) long.

Range: Oceans worldwide.

Habitat: Surface waters.

What it eats: Zooplankton, other comb jellies.

What eats it: Fish, sea turtles, jellyfish, other comb jellies.

Appeared on Earth: Possibly more than 550 million years ago.

Lifespan: A few weeks to 3 years.

Sponge

Scientific name: *Porifera* (pore bearer). There are more than 9,000 species of sponge.

Size: The smallest sponges are the size of a quarter, and the largest is as big as a car.

Range: Oceans and fresh water worldwide.

Habitat: Most sponges live in the ocean from the Arctic to the tropics, but about 150 species live in fresh water.

What it eats: Plankton, bacteria, and marine snow (bits of dead animal and plant matter).

What eats it: Sea turtles, snails.

Appeared on Earth: 600 million years ago.

Lifespan: Some sponges can live more than 2,000 years.

DIVE DEEPER!
Learn More About Evolution and Extreme Survivors

Online

Ology: The American Museum of Natural History's Website for Kids
http://www.amnh.org/explore/ology
Fun and informative site exploring sciences from anthropology through zoology through loads of activities, videos, and more.

Understanding Evolution, University of California Museum of Paleontology
evolution.berkeley.edu

The Horseshoe Crab
http://horseshoecrab.org/
A comprehensive website including everything from natural history, research, and conservation to teaching resources and poems.

The International Society of Tardigrade Hunters
http://tardigradehunters.weebly.com/
How to find tardigrades, interviews with scientists, and more.

Smithsonian National Museum of Natural History Ocean Portal
https://ocean.si.edu/
A great, searchable site with articles, news, and resources for educators.

Books

Billions of Years, Amazing Changes: The Story of Evolution, by Laurence Pringle, Boyds Mills Press, 2011.

Evolution, by Linda Gamlin, DK Eyewitness Books, 2009.

Grandmother Fish: A Child's First Book of Evolution, by Jonathan Tweet and Karen Lewis, Feiwel & Friends/MacMillan, 2016.

Life on Earth: The Story of Evolution, by Steve Jenkins, Houghton Mifflin, 2002.

Living Fossils: Clues to the Past, by Caroline Arnold, Charlesbridge, 2016.

Selected Bibliography

Cramer, Deborah. *The Narrow Edge: A Tiny Bird, An Ancient Crab & an Epic Journey*, Yale University Press, 2015.

Darwin, Charles. *The Origin of Species,* Random House, 1979.

Dawkins, Richard and Wong, Yan. *The Ancestor's Tale: A Pilgrimage to the Dawn of Evolution*, Second Edition, Mariner Books, Houghton Mifflin Harcourt, 2016.

Fortey, Richard. *Survivors: The Animals and Plants that Time Has Left Behind,* HarperCollins, 2011.

Naskrecki, Piotr. *Relics: Travels in Nature's Time Machine,* University of Chicago Press, 2011.

Glossary

bacteria: (singular, *bacterium*) Microscopic, singled-celled organisms that are able to eat and rapidly multiply. More bacteria live on Earth than any other living thing. Some cause disease, but most help digest food and break down waste into chemicals and nutrients.

cephalopod: A class of mollusks that that includes nautiluses, octopuses, squid, and cuttlefish. Cephalopod means "head foot." These marine animals all have tentacles or "feet" growing out of their heads.

cilia: (singular, cilium) Tiny, hair-like structures that often form a fringe. Comb jellies and certain other organism pulse their cilia in unison to propel themselves through the water.

crustacean: An animal with a tough outer covering (called an exoskeleton), antennae, and jointed legs. Tadpole shrimp are crustaceans as are crabs, lobsters, shrimp, and amphipods.

cryptobiosis: A reversible state in which a tardigrade's body functions stop in response to harsh conditions. It means "hidden life."

cysts: The eggs of tadpole shrimp and fairy shrimp, which can survive extreme conditions such as drought for years before hatching.

DNA: The molecule inside the cells of all organisms that contains their genetic instructions. It is an abbreviation for *deoxyribonucleic acid*.

estivation: An inactive state that some animals in hot climates enter in summer to survive extreme heat or drought.

evolution: The gradual change in organisms over generations during the history of the Earth. It often results in new species.

exoskeleton: A hard, jointed covering that protects invertebrates such as horseshoe crabs, insects, and crustaceans.

extinct: No longer existing. An organism becomes extinct when it dies off and there are no more of its kind on the Earth. It is a natural part of evolution. More than 99 percent of all life forms that have ever existed have become extinct.

fossil: remains and tracks of animals preserved in stone.

gene: a unit of DNA that is passed from parents to offspring. Genes control the development of features or "traits," such as eye color and height in humans.

habitat: the place where an animal, plant, or other organism naturally lives.

hibernation: An inactive state that some animals enter in cold climates in winter.

hypothesis: An early explanation for an observation or scientific problem that can be tested by investigation though experimentation and study.

invertebrate: an animal that doesn't have a backbone, such as an insect or worm.

LAL: An abbreviation for *Limulus Amebocyte Lysate*, a substance extracted from the blood cells of horseshoe crabs. It clots around bacteria and is used to test medical supplies such as needles and intravenous drugs for safety.

metabolism: The processes by which living things turn food into energy, build tissue, and eliminate waste.

natural selection: A process in which organisms best adapted to their environments survive and reproduce, passing their characteristics to their offspring. Over time and through many generations, this process can lead to new species. Natural selection is the main driver of evolution.

nocturnal: Active mainly at night.

offspring: An animal's children.

organism: a living thing.

ornithologist: a scientist who studies birds.

paleontologist: a scientist who studies fossils.

plankton: (singular, *plankter*) Microscopic plants and tiny animals that drift in the ocean and fresh water.

scavenger: an animal that feeds on dead organisms or waste.

siphuncle: a tube that runs through the compartments of a nautilus's shell. It allows a nautilus to raise or lower itself in the water column by adjusting the mix of seawater and gas inside its shell.

spawn: to lay eggs. Refers to fish and other aquatic animals.

species: groups of organisms that look alike and can reproduce.

tetrapod: Any vertebrate with two pairs of limbs, such as humans and dogs.

tun: The dormant state of a tardigrade.

zooplankton: tiny and microscopic animals that live in water.

ACKNOWLEDGMENTS

Thanks to Dr. Joel Carlin, Biology Department Chair, Gustavus Adolphus College, and Dr. David Porter, Professor Emeritus, Department of Plant Biology, University of Georgia, for reviewing the text and generously sharing their expertise. Thanks to Dr. Thomas C. Boothby for his expertise on tardigrades and how to find them. Any errors are my own. A deep bow of thanks to my writers' group—Ellen Booraem, Jean Fogelberg, Lisa Heldke, Ann Logan, Becky McCall, Gail Page, and Susa Wuorinen—for their careful critiques, good humor, and encouragement. Deepest gratitude to my husband Thomas Curry, who has cheerfully weathered a deluge of "fun facts" about sea sponges, comb jellies, and other extreme survivors.

ABOUT THE AUTHOR

KIMBERLY RIDLEY is a science writer and editor whose articles and essays have appeared in the *Boston Globe*, *The Christian Science Monitor*, and many other print and online publications. Her children's books include the multi-award winning *The Secret Pool* (*Kirkus* starred review) and *The Secret Bay*, both of which won the Riverby Award for "outstanding natural history books for young people" from the John Burroughs Association. She holds an M.S. in Science Journalism from Boston University and loves visiting schools to share her passions for science and writing nonfiction. www.kimridley.com

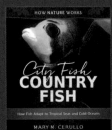

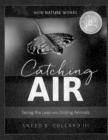

HOW NATURE WORKS

HOW NATURE WORKS books don't just catalog the natural world in beautiful photographs. They seek to understand why nature functions as it does. They ask questions, and they encourage readers to ask more. They explore nature's mysteries, sharing what we know and celebrating what we have yet to discover. Other HOW NATURE WORKS books include:

Catching Air: Taking the Leap with Gliding Animals

978-0-8848-496-7

City Fish, Country Fish: How Fish Adapt to Tropical Seas and Cold Oceans

978-0-88448-529-2